CONTENTS

Words in **bold** can be found in the Glossary on page 22.

Ducks on the farm

Do you know where the soft feathers in a snuggly feather pillow and **duvet** come from? Many of these feathers come from ducks.

A mother duck swimming with her ducklings.

A group of Aylesbury ducks.

Ducks are found on farms all around the world. They are very useful birds. They give us meat, eggs and feathers. Ducks can help farmers, too. They gobble up lots of slugs and snails that like to eat the farmers' crops.

Ducks from beak to tail

The largest ducks can grow up to 40cm long, from shoulder to tail, and can weigh as much as 6kg. That's the same weight as six bags of sugar.

Eye

Body covered in feathers

Wings for flying

Beak

Tail

Webbed feet for swimming

This drake has curly tail feathers.

Height of six-year-old child

FARM FACT
Not all ducks quack! Only female ducks make a quacking sound. The drake makes a squeaky noise.

Male ducks are called **drakes**, female ducks are called ducks and baby ducks are called **ducklings**.

Height of duck

Some drakes are more colourful than ducks, and have curly feathers on their tails.

7

It's a duck's life...

A duck starts life inside an egg. The female duck lays eggs in a nest, then she sits on them to keep them warm.

The ducklings **hatch** after 28 days. Each duckling makes a hole in its shell with a special egg tooth at the end of its beak. It cracks open the shell and pushes itself out. A duckling can run around within minutes of hatching.

These newly hatched ducklings have fluffy feathers.

Ducklings replace their fluffy feathers with stiff adult feathers when they grow up.

FARM FACT
Some ducks live for a long time. One white drake living in Wales reached the amazing age of 25!

A baby duck has all its grown-up feathers by the time it is about seven weeks old.

A female duck starts to lay eggs during her first spring. Ducks can live for between two and 15 years, depending on how many eggs they lay.

Dabbling ducks

Ducks like to play in mud and make a mess! They push their beaks into the mud to look for small animals to eat, such as worms and snails.

Ducks also love swimming. They have large **webbed** feet that are perfect for paddling around in water.

Ducks cannot feel the cold through their feet.

Sometimes a duck bobs up and down on the water with its head under the surface and its tail in the air. This is called **dabbling**.

A duck dabbles so that its head can reach the bottom of the pond to look for food.

11

Eggs and meat

Female ducks lay large white eggs. They are about twice the size of hen eggs. Most ducks lay their eggs during spring and summer, although some lay eggs all year round.

A good egg-laying duck may lay more than 300 eggs in a year! Duck eggs can be eaten, just like hen eggs.

Duck eggs can be used to make yummy cakes.

12

Duck is popular in Chinese cooking.

FARM FACT
The number of eggs a duck lays depends on the amount of daylight the duck gets. The more daylight – the more eggs!

Some types of duck grow very large, such as the Aylesbury and Peking ducks. These ducks are kept for meat in special farms. There are lots of these farms in South-East Asia and China. These ducks grow quickly and can get very fat!

Wonderfully warm

A mallard drake in flight.

A duck has different types of feathers. It has a layer of smooth feathers that covers its body. The long feathers on its wings are called flight feathers. They help a duck to fly. Small fluffy feathers called down feathers lie next to a duck's skin.

An eiderdown is a type of duvet filled with down feathers. It is named after the Eider duck.

The Eider is a wild duck that lives in cold places where temperatures fall below freezing. It has very, very warm feathers!

15

Different ducks

INDIAN RUNNER

This is a tall duck that stands very upright. It is nicknamed the 'penguin duck' because it stands a bit like a penguin.

MAYA

The Maya duck comes from China. Flocks of Maya ducks are herded onto fields of rice. The ducks feed on insects and other small animals living around the rice, to help protect the crops from harm.

MAGPIE DUCK

This duck has white feathers with blue-grey patches on its head and body. It lays blue eggs.

CRESTED DUCK

The **crested** duck has a puff of feathers that sticks up on its head. Some look like they are wearing little hats! Crested ducks come in different colours.

17

Duck customs

KOREA

It is a **tradition** in Korea to give a pair of **carved** ducks as a wedding present for good luck. If the married couple is happy, they place the ducks so they face each other. If they are unhappy, the ducks look away from each other.

SINGAPORE

Many people around the world hold duck races. In Singapore, plastic ducks are let go on a river and float **downstream**. The owner of the duck that crosses the finishing line first wins a prize.

18

CHINA

Each autumn, Chinese people celebrate the Moon Festival. It is traditional to eat Moon Cakes during the festival. There are different types of Moon Cakes, but one type has a cooked duck egg yolk inside. People eat the cakes at night, under a full moon.

19

Quacking good fun

Make your own colourful duck. You will need a paper plate, an A4 sheet of yellow paper, an A4 sheet of orange card, pencil, paints, paintbrush, scissors, glue, feathers (optional) and a black pen.

1 Paint one side of the paper plate yellow and fold it in half. The yellow colour should be on the outside. Press firmly along the fold.

2 Place the sheet of yellow paper on a table and trace around your hand twice with a pencil.

3 Ask a grown-up to cut out the two hand shapes. These shapes form the tail feathers. Glue them into position on each side of the plate.

4 Draw a beak and legs with webbed feet on the orange card. Ask a grown-up to cut them out for you. Glue the beak and the legs to the plate.

5 Paint wings on both sides of the plate. Stick any feathers you have onto the wings. Draw on two eyes with black pen.

Glossary and Index

carved shaped by cutting with a knife or sharp blade

crest feathers that stick up on the head of a duck

dabbling when ducks push their beaks into mud under water to look for food

downstream the direction in which the water in a river or stream flows

drake a male duck

duckling a baby duck

duvet a large bed cover, filled with feathers, that keeps you warm at night

gland part of a duck's body that makes special oil which the duck uses to make its feathers waterproof

hatch when a duckling breaks out of its egg

preening when a duck cleans its feathers with its beak

tradition a custom or way of doing something that is passed from parent to child

vertically straight up or down

webbed joined by pieces of skin, that make it easy to swim

Ideas for teachers and parents

- Read about the different breeds of duck. Make factsheets about the children's favourite breeds. Find out which ones are used for meat and which ones are kept for eggs.

- Visit a waterfowl or poultry centre where children can see different breeds of duck. A good time to visit is late spring or early summer when there will be ducklings as well as adult ducks. Some centres allow children to go into the incubator rooms to see ducklings hatch.

- Visit local ponds with the children to see wild ducks.

- Have a look inside a pillow containing feathers. Take one of the feathers and look at how it is constructed. Puff up the duck-down pillow or duvet to show how duvets and pillows trap air and help keep you warm.

- Make a collage of a duck. Take a large piece of white paper and draw the outline of a duck on it. Look through old magazines and cut out any pictures of ducks, ducklings and feathers. Collect scraps of material and natural or artificial feathers. Stick these onto the outline to make a colourful duck.

- Make a wordsearch using the duck-related vocabulary in this book.

- Compare duck eggs with hen eggs. Duck eggs can be bought in some supermarkets or from farm shops. Weigh a duck egg. See how easy it is to break the egg open. Compare the weight and ease of breaking with a hen egg. Make two lots of scrambled eggs, one with duck eggs and one with hen eggs. Ask the children if they can taste any difference.

- Ask the children to think of the names of famous ducks that appear in books, poems and cartoons, for example Jemima Puddle-duck or Donald Duck. Encourage them to write a poem about a duck.

PLEASE NOTE

- Check that each child does not have an egg intolerance before carrying out the scrambled egg activity above.

24